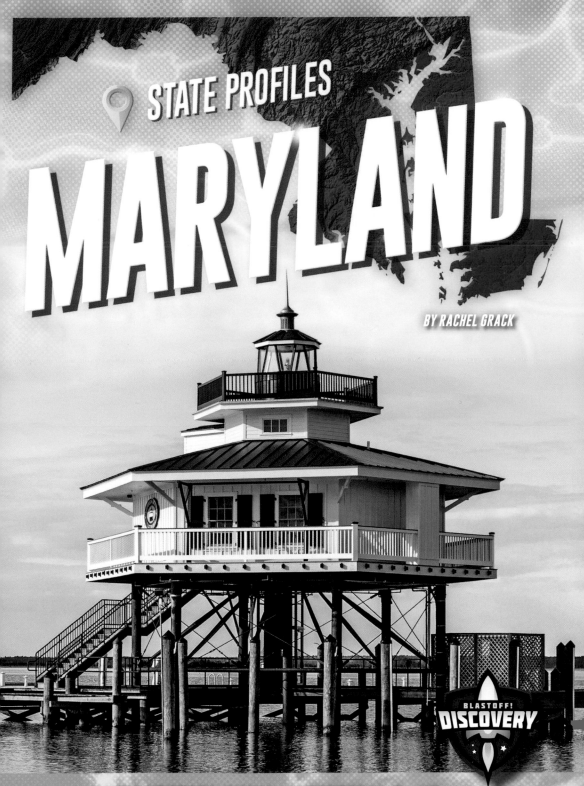

STATE PROFILES

MARYLAND

BY RACHEL GRACK

BLASTOFF! DISCOVERY

BELLWETHER MEDIA • MINNEAPOLIS, MN

Blastoff! Discovery launches a new mission: reading to learn. Filled with facts and features, each book offers you an exciting new world to explore!

BLASTOFF! UNIVERSE

BLASTOFF! Beginners — GRADE K

BLASTOFF! READERS — GRADES 1-3

BLASTOFF! DISCOVERY — GRADE 4

This edition first published in 2022 by Bellwether Media, Inc.

No part of this publication may be reproduced in whole or in part without written permission of the publisher.
For information regarding permission, write to Bellwether Media, Inc., Attention: Permissions Department,
6012 Blue Circle Drive, Minnetonka, MN 55343.

Library of Congress Cataloging-in-Publication Data

Names: Koestler-Grack, Rachel A., 1973- author.
Title: Maryland / by Rachel Grack.
Description: Minneapolis, MN : Bellwether Media, 2022. |
    Series: Blastoff! Discovery: State profiles | Includes bibliographical
    references and index. | Audience: Ages 7-13 | Audience: Grades
    4-6 | Summary: "Engaging images accompany information
    about Maryland. The combination of high-interest subject matter
    and narrative text is intended for students in grades 3 through 8"
    Provided by publisher.
Identifiers: LCCN 2021019697 (print) | LCCN 2021019698 (ebook)
    | ISBN 9781644873915 (library binding) |
    ISBN 9781648341687 (ebook)
Subjects: LCSH: Maryland–Juvenile literature.
Classification: LCC F181.3 .G73 2022 (print) | LCC F181.3 (ebook)
    | DDC 975.2–dc23
LC record available at https://lccn.loc.gov/2021019697
LC ebook record available at https://lccn.loc.gov/2021019698

Editor: Betsy Rathburn   Designer: Andrea Schneider

Printed in the United States of America, North Mankato, MN.

 # TABLE OF CONTENTS

Swallow Falls State Park	4
Where Is Maryland?	6
Maryland's Beginnings	8
Landscape and Climate	10
Wildlife	12
People and Communities	14
Baltimore	16
Industry	18
Food	20
Sports and Entertainment	22
Festivals and Traditions	24
Maryland Timeline	26
Maryland Facts	28
Glossary	30
To Learn More	31
Index	32

YOUGHIOGHENY RIVER
SWALLOW FALLS STATE PARK

A family is spending the day at Swallow Falls State Park. They take a hike down a trail into the forest. Oak, maple, and pine trees line the trail. Their branches spread out overhead to provide shade. As the family hikes, they stop along the way to admire the Upper Swallow Falls along the Youghiogheny River.

ANTIETAM NATIONAL BATTLEFIELD

ASSATEAGUE ISLAND

CALVERT CLIFFS STATE PARK

NATIONAL AQUARIUM

They continue walking and soon reach Muddy Creek Falls. This waterfall tumbles 53 feet (16 meters) over a rocky cliff! The family hikes all the way to the bottom of its tumbling waters. They carefully step onto some rocks to get a closer look. Welcome to Maryland!

5

N
W ⊕ E
S

Maryland lies on the East Coast of the United States. It covers 12,406 square miles (32,131 square kilometers), making it the ninth smallest state. Maryland shares its long, straight northern border with Pennsylvania. Delaware is to the north and east. The Potomac River separates Maryland from Virginia and West Virginia to the southwest. Along the Virginia border, Maryland surrounds Washington, D.C., on three sides.

The Chesapeake Bay cuts deep into Maryland. The state capital, Annapolis, sits on its western shore. East of the bay, a small section of Maryland's eastern border touches the Atlantic Ocean.

WEST
VIRGINIA

PENNSYLVANIA

MARYLAND

GERMANTOWN • • BALTIMORE

COLUMBIA

WASHINGTON, D.C. •

☆ ANNAPOLIS

DELAWARE

POTOMAC
RIVER

VIRGINIA

CHESAPEAKE
BAY

ATLANTIC
OCEAN

PAN-SHAPED STATE

Western Maryland is often
called the state's panhandle
because of its shape.

CIVIL WAR

ST. MARY'S CITY

At least 10,000 years ago, Paleo-Indians arrived in present-day Maryland. In time, many Native American tribes formed. These included the Nanticoke, Piscataway, Choptank, Delaware, Matapeake, and various Iroquois groups.

In 1632, England established Maryland as a **colony**. The colony's first capital was St. Mary's City. Starting in 1775, Marylanders fought for independence from Britain in the **Revolutionary War**. Maryland became the seventh state in 1788. In the 1860s, Maryland fought as a part of the United States during the **Civil War**. Many important battles took place in the state.

NATIVE PEOPLES OF MARYLAND

PISCATAWAY INDIAN NATION

- Original lands west of the Chesapeake Bay to the Potomac River
- Around 100 members in Maryland today

ACCOHANNOCK INDIAN TRIBE

- Original lands in eastern Virginia
- Around 100 members in Maryland today

PISCATAWAY CONOY TRIBE

- Original lands west of the Chesapeake Bay to the Potomac River
- Around 3,500 members in southern Maryland today

Western Maryland is covered by the Appalachian Mountains. These tree-covered hills and rocky peaks stretch eastward into central Maryland. The mountains flatten into the Piedmont, which stretches into northeastern Maryland. From there, a marshy coastal **plain** stretches to the Atlantic Ocean. Sandy beaches run along the coast. Many islands dot the coastline.

APPALACHIAN MOUNTAINS ■ PIEDMONT
COASTAL PLAIN

N
W E
S

DEEP CREEK LAKE

LACK OF LAKES

Maryland's lakes are all human-made. The largest is Deep Creek Lake in western Maryland. It has over 60 miles (97 kilometers) of shoreline!

SPRING
HIGH: 65°F (18°C)
LOW: 44°F (7°C)

SUMMER
HIGH: 86°F (30°C)
LOW: 66°F (19°C)

FALL
HIGH: 88°F (20°C)
LOW: 49°F (9°C)

WINTER
HIGH: 45°F (7°C)
LOW: 28°F (-2°C)

°F = degrees Fahrenheit
°C = degrees Celsius

Eastern Maryland has hot summers with thunderstorms and hailstorms. Coastal **hurricanes** sometimes bring heavy rains and flooding. Summers in the mountains are cooler. But winters last longer and get heavier snowfall than the coast.

11

In Maryland's Appalachian Mountains, black bears search for nuts, berries, and seeds. Red foxes, gray squirrels, and Virginia opossums scurry through the forests. Overhead, owls, sparrows, and woodpeckers perch in the tall trees.

Box turtles and snapping turtles swim through Maryland's rivers and wetlands. Frogs and salamanders creep through marsh grasses, while herons wade nearby. The waters of the Chesapeake Bay are home to eels, catfish, and even sharks. In the winter, nearly 1 million ducks, swans, and geese spend the season in the bay. Sea turtles, bottlenose dolphins, and humpback whales are often spotted along Maryland's Atlantic Coast.

BLACK BEAR

BARRED OWL

COMMON SNAPPING TURTLE

BOTTLENOSE DOLPHIN

MARYLAND'S FUTURE: CLIMATE CHANGE

Climate change is affecting Maryland's wildlife. Experts predict sea levels may rise several feet by the year 2100. This will destroy animal homes in coastal areas. Many birds and fish are threatened by the change.

BLUE CRAB

Life Span: up to 4 years
Status: least concern

blue crab range =

LEAST CONCERN	NEAR THREATENED	VULNERABLE	ENDANGERED	CRITICALLY ENDANGERED	EXTINCT IN THE WILD	EXTINCT

More than 6 million people live in Maryland. Its large population and small size give it a high **population density**. Most Marylanders live in **urban** areas. Many people live in or near Maryland's largest city, Baltimore. Some **suburbs** of Washington, D.C., are also in Maryland.

FREDERICK DOUGLASS

Frederick Douglass was born a slave in Maryland. He escaped slavery and became a writer, speaker, and leader in the fight to end slavery.

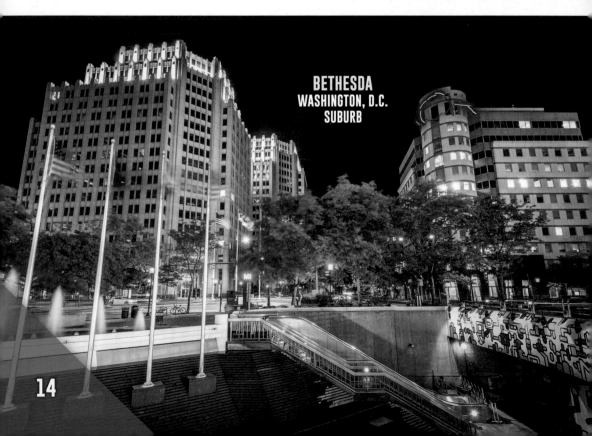

BETHESDA
WASHINGTON, D.C.
SUBURB

FAMOUS MARYLANDER

Name: Cal Ripken Jr.

Born: August 24, 1960

Hometown: Havre de Grace, Maryland

Famous For: Baseball player for the Baltimore Orioles, where he played a record 2,632 back-to-back games and was eventually added to the Baseball Hall of Fame

Around 6 out of 10 Marylanders have European **ancestors**. About 3 out of 10 Marylanders are African American or Black. The next-largest groups are people with Hispanic or Asian backgrounds. Small Native American populations live in Maryland's cities and towns. Many of Maryland's new **immigrants** are from El Salvador. Others come from India, China, and Nigeria.

Baltimore was founded in 1729. Its location on the Chesapeake Bay soon made it an important port city. The city shipped tobacco and grain. It was also a shipbuilding center. Later, railroads helped boost steel, oil, and other industries.

THE LUMBEE TRIBE

Starting in the early 1900s, many members of the Lumbee tribe began moving to Maryland from North Carolina. Most moved to Baltimore. Today, a community of about 2,000 Lumbee still lives in the city!

Today, Baltimore is Maryland's largest city. It is still a major seaport. Many automobiles are shipped from the port. Baltimore is also a **cultural** center. People visit the Reginald F. Lewis Museum to learn about the history of African Americans in Baltimore. People shop, eat, and stroll past historic ships along Baltimore's Inner Harbor. At the National Aquarium, visitors can see many different sea creatures!

NATIONAL AQUARIUM

INNER HARBOR

Farming was one of Maryland's most important early industries. Farmers grew tobacco, wheat, and corn. Grain **mills** along the Chesapeake Bay turned wheat and corn into flour. By the 1800s, **manufacturing** boomed. Many factories made parts for ships. Coal mining in western Maryland was also important.

MARYLAND'S CHALLENGE: TEACHERS NEEDED

Maryland faces a teacher shortage. Fewer teachers are moving to Maryland from other states. Fewer Marylanders are becoming teachers. Current teachers are finding other careers. Maryland hopes to fix the problem by paying teachers more.

Today, Maryland's top manufactured goods are electronics, processed foods, and chemical products. The state's fishing industry brings in money from blue crabs, oysters, and fish. Timber is also important. Most Marylanders have **service jobs**. Many work in stores, restaurants, or hospitals.

INVENTED IN MARYLAND

FIRST GAS STREET LAMP

Date Invented: 1816
Inventor: Rembrandt Peale

BOTTLE CAP

Date Invented: 1892
Inventor: William Painter

FIRST DENTAL SCHOOL

Date Founded: 1940
Founded By: Horace Hayden and Chapin Harris

CORDLESS DRILL

Date Invented: 1961
Inventor: Black & Decker

SOFT-SHELL CRAB

CRAB SEASON

Summertime is soft-shell crab season in Maryland. This is the time of year when crabs shed their shells. People can eat the whole crab without needing to crack the shell!

Many Maryland dishes are centered on seafood. Blue crab is often steamed and sprinkled with Old Bay, a seasoning invented in Maryland. Crab cakes and fried rockfish are also popular. At summer oyster roasts, Marylanders roast fresh oysters over open fires.

FRIED ROCKFISH

SMITH ISLAND CAKE

Pit beef sandwiches were created in Maryland. Beef is roasted, sliced, and topped with horseradish and onion, then served on a bun. Maryland-style chicken, fried chicken topped with white gravy, is another state favorite. Smith Island cake is Maryland's state dessert. Many thin layers of cake are stacked with chocolate frosting. Chocolate-covered Berger cookies are another favorite treat!

BERGER COOKIES

24 SERVINGS

Have an adult help you make this recipe.

INGREDIENTS

1/3 cup butter
1 teaspoon vanilla
1 teaspoon baking powder
1/2 cup sugar
1 large egg
1½ cups flour
1/3 cup milk
16-ounce container of chocolate fudge frosting

DIRECTIONS

1. Preheat oven to 400 degrees Fahrenheit (204 degrees Celsius).
2. Line a baking sheet with parchment paper.
3. In a large bowl, combine butter, vanilla, baking powder, and sugar. Mix until creamy.
4. Add egg. Beat until mixed together.
5. Slowly add flour and milk. Beat until well mixed.
6. Scoop spoonfuls of dough onto the baking sheet about two inches apart. Flatten cookies slightly.
8. Bake cookies 8 to 10 minutes. Cool on a wire rack.
9. When cooled, spread each cookie with a thick layer of frosting.

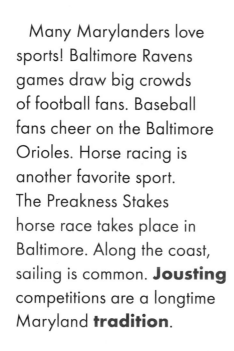

PREAKNESS STAKES

Many Marylanders love sports! Baltimore Ravens games draw big crowds of football fans. Baseball fans cheer on the Baltimore Orioles. Horse racing is another favorite sport. The Preakness Stakes horse race takes place in Baltimore. Along the coast, sailing is common. **Jousting** competitions are a longtime Maryland **tradition**.

STATE CHAMPS

Maryland is home to champion sports teams. The Orioles won their third World Series in 1983. The Ravens won their second Super Bowl in 2013!

Maryland's museums attract visitors interested in art and history. People visit performing arts centers to see plays and concerts. Maryland's state parks attract hikers and campers. Along the coast, people swim and sunbathe at state beaches. Many visit Assateague Island to see the famous wild horses!

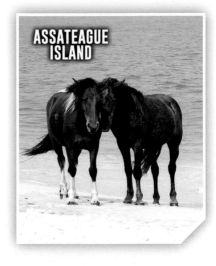

ASSATEAGUE ISLAND

NOTABLE SPORTS TEAM

Baltimore Orioles
Sport: Major League Baseball
Started: 1901 (1954 in Baltimore)
Place of Play: Oriole Park at Camden Yards

Many Maryland festivals celebrate the state's rich culture. Every July, the Caribbean Carnival brings Caribbean food, dancing, and music to Baltimore. In August, the AFRAM Festival celebrates African American history and culture. The Baltimore American Indian Center **Powwow** welcomes visitors to enjoy traditional music, dancing, and drumming each fall.

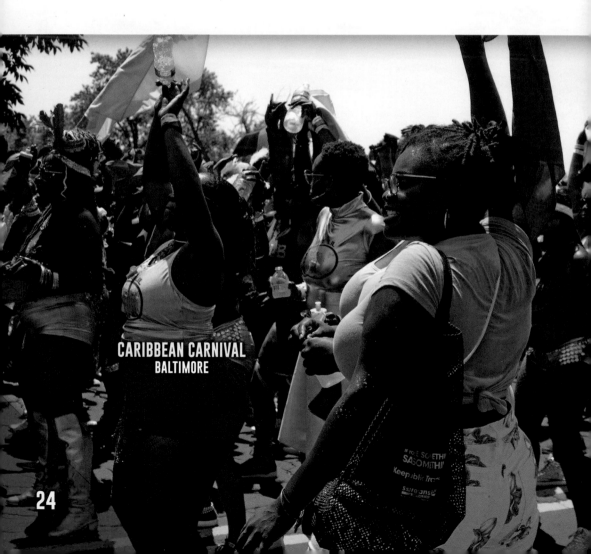

CARIBBEAN CARNIVAL
BALTIMORE

NATIONAL HARD
CRAB DERBY
CRISFIELD

Food festivals are also popular. Crisfield ends the summer with the National Hard Crab Derby. People gather to watch crab races, see fireworks, and taste crab recipes. In the fall, the Maryland Seafood Festival draws thousands of people to Annapolis. They taste crab soups, listen to music, and play games. There is a lot to celebrate in Maryland!

MARYLAND
SEAFOOD
FESTIVAL

1632

Maryland becomes a colony of England

1500s

Europeans explore the Chesapeake Bay

1788

Maryland becomes the seventh U.S. state after the Revolutionary War

1729

Baltimore is founded

1862

The Battle of Antietam is fought in Maryland during the Civil War

2013

The Baltimore
Ravens win the
Super Bowl

1967

Marylander Thurgood
Marshall becomes the first
African American member
of the U.S. Supreme Court

2012

Maryland recognizes
the Piscataway Indian
Nation and Piscataway
Conoy Tribe

1966

The Baltimore Orioles win
their first World Series

2017

Maryland recognizes
the Accohannock Tribe

Nicknames: Old Line State, Free State

Motto: *Fatti Maschii Parole Femine*
(Strong Deeds, Gentle Words)

Date of Statehood: April 28, 1788 (the 7th state)

Capital City: Annapolis ★

Other Major Cities: Baltimore, Columbia, Germantown

Area: 12,407 square miles (32,134 square kilometers);
Maryland is the 42nd largest state.

Population

6,177,224
(2020)

STATE FLAG

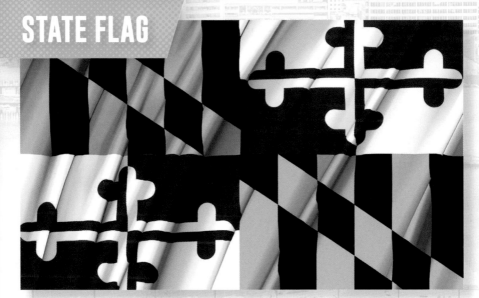

Maryland's flag is based on the coat of arms of the Calvert family, a well-known family from the state's early history. The flag is divided into quarters. The top left and bottom right are a black and gold design. The top right and bottom left are a red and white cross design. During the Civil War, many Marylanders flew the red and white design to show they supported the Confederacy. The black and gold design became a symbol of Maryland's place in the Union. In 1904, the two designs were combined to make Maryland's flag.

INDUSTRY

JOBS

- MANUFACTURING **3%**
- FARMING AND NATURAL RESOURCES **3%**
- GOVERNMENT **16%**
- SERVICES **78%**

Main Exports

natural gas

chemicals

automobiles

aircraft and engine parts

Natural Resources
lumber, seafood, natural gas, coal, crushed stone, limestone

GOVERNMENT

10 ELECTORAL VOTES

Federal Government
8 REPRESENTATIVES | **2** SENATORS

MD

USA

State Government
141 REPRESENTATIVES | **47** SENATORS

STATE SYMBOLS

STATE BIRD
BALTIMORE ORIOLE

STATE CRUSTACEAN
BLUE CRAB

STATE FLOWER
BLACK-EYED SUSAN

STATE TREE
WHITE OAK

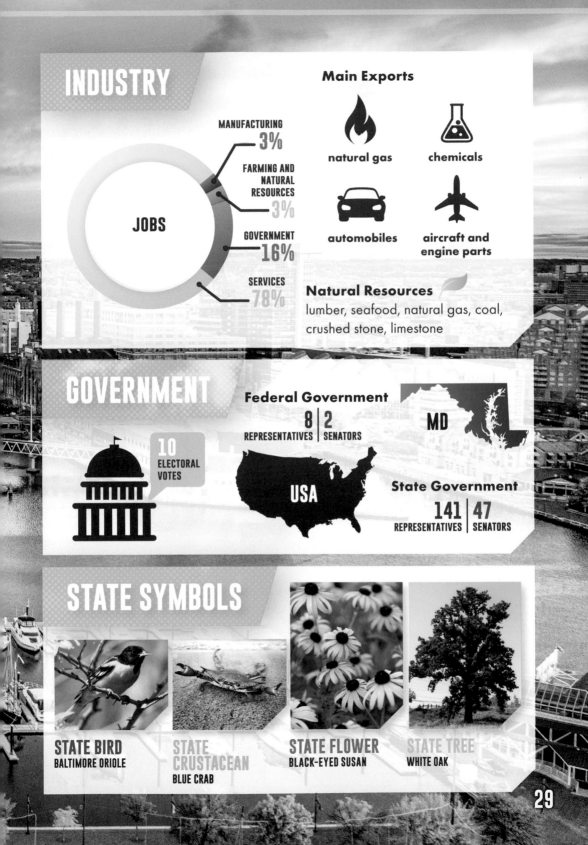

GLOSSARY

ancestors—relatives who lived long ago

Civil War—a war between the Northern (Union) and Southern (Confederate) states that lasted from 1861 to 1865

colony—a distant territory which is under the control of another nation

cultural—relating to the beliefs, arts, and ways of life in a place or society

hurricanes—storms formed in the tropics that have violent winds and often have rain and lightning

immigrants—people who move to a new country

jousting—a sport played on horseback with long poles called lances

manufacturing—a field of work in which people use machines to make products

mills—buildings with machines for processing materials; mills produce materials such as lumber and flour.

plain—a large area of flat land

population density—a measure of how crowded a place is based on the number of people per square mile

powwow—a Native American gathering that usually includes dancing

Revolutionary War—the war from 1775 to 1783 in which the United States fought for independence from Great Britain

service jobs—jobs that perform tasks for people or businesses

suburbs—the towns and communities just outside of a large city

tradition—a custom, idea, or belief handed down from one generation to the next

urban—related to cities and city life

AT THE LIBRARY

Bailey, Diane. *The Story of the Baltimore Ravens.* Minneapolis, Minn.: Kaleidoscope, 2020.

Miller, Derek. *Maryland.* New York, N.Y.: Cavendish Square, 2019.

Prince, April Jones. *Who Was Frederick Douglass?* New York, N.Y.: Grosset & Dunlap, 2014.

ON THE WEB

FACTSURFER

Factsurfer.com gives you a safe, fun way to find more information.

1. Go to www.factsurfer.com.

2. Enter "Maryland" into the search box and click 🔍.

3. Select your book cover to see a list of related content.

AFRAM Festival, 24
Annapolis, 6, 7, 25
arts, 17, 23, 24
Baltimore, 7, 14, 16–17, 24
Baltimore American Indian
    Center Powwow, 24
Baltimore Orioles, 15, 22, 23
capital (see Annapolis)
Caribbean Carnival, 24
Chesapeake Bay, 6, 7, 12, 16
Civil War, 8, 9
climate, 11, 12
Douglass, Frederick, 14
fast facts, 28–29
festivals, 24–25
food, 20–21, 25
future, 12, 18
history, 8–9, 16, 18

inventions, 19
landmarks, 5, 17, 23
landscape, 10–11, 12
location, 6–7
Maryland Seafood Festival, 25
National Hard Crab Derby, 25
outdoor activities, 17, 22, 23
people, 8, 9, 14–15, 16, 24
Rathbun, Mary Jane, 13
recipe, 21
Revolutionary War, 9
Ripken Jr., Cal, 15
size, 6
sports, 22, 23
Swallow Falls State Park, 4–5
timeline, 26–27
wildlife, 12–13
working, 16, 17, 18–19